A BATTLE OF WORDS

Heather Christie

Illustrated by Jacqui Young

Written by Heather Christie
Illustrated by Jacqui Young
Designed by Marina Messiha

Published by Mimosa Publications Pty Ltd
PO Box 779, Hawthorn 3122, Australia
© 1995 Mimosa Publications Pty Ltd

Distributed in the United Kingdom by
Kingscourt Publishing Limited
PO Box 1427, London W6 9BR, England

Distributed in Australia by
Rigby Heinemann
(a division of Reed International Books Australia Pty Ltd)
22 Salmon Street, Port Melbourne, Victoria 3207

Distributed in New Zealand by
Shortland Publications Limited
2B Cawley Street, Ellerslie, Auckland

03 02 01 00 99
10 9 8 7 6 5 4
Printed in Hong Kong through Bookbuilders Ltd

ISBN 0 7327 1546 6

A BATTLE OF WORDS

A BATTLE OF WORDS

It all began with my birthday present – a great pair of in-line skates. I just couldn't wait to race out and try them – but then, before I knew it, I was accused of – oh, never mind. You read the letters and decide who was right and who was wrong in this battle of words.

16 The Crescent
September 15

To the Young Female Person residing
at 18 The Crescent,

This afternoon, at approximately 4:10
p.m.(I was much too shaken to note
the exact time), you EXPLODED from
your gate. In your mad rush,
a hard object struck me, causing me
to drop my shopping. My carton of
milk burst. This resulted in my:
(a)Having to hose down the pavement
(b)Having to wash all the articles
   of shopping
(c)NOT having any milk.

So what do we have?
(a)A waste of water
(b)A waste of time
(c)A waste of milk.

But that's not all. I was looking
forward to a well-earned cup of tea.
I have never drunk, nor will I ever
drink, my tea without milk!

Yours faithfully,

C. V. Molesworth

C. V. Molesworth
(Resident and rate-payer)

"Better let me check that letter to C. V. Molesworth," Dad suggested, when he saw me writing a reply. Dad is a court reporter; he knows about "incriminating statements" and things like that.

"P. S. can return some milk," Mum said. "I'll buy a carton to replace the one that she spilt."

"*If* P. S. did spill the milk in the first place," Dad said. "We don't know that she did. We only have C. V. Molesworth's word on that."

"For goodness' sake," Mum said. "What's a little milk? All this will blow over once C. V. Molesworth has had a nice cup of tea."

18 The Crescent
September 15

Dear C. V. Molesworth,

The carton of milk that comes with this letter does not mean that I admit I am guilty. Mum just thought you'd like a cup of tea.

I'm sorry you've had so much trouble. The "hard object" you mention might have been my elbow. If it was, I'm very sorry, even though there is NO EVIDENCE that this *was* the "hard object".

Dad says that if I hit you with my elbow I would have felt it. Mum says that I don't feel, see, or hear *anything* when I'm excited. I was trying out my new birthday present, you see.

Yours faithfully,

P. S. McGinnity

P. S. McGinnity (Resident and non rate-payer)

We haven't lived at 18 The Crescent very long. It was a "deceased estate". That means the person living here before us died. Mum says he was an old gentleman and it all became too much for him. When Dad tries to cut down the undergrowth, he mutters that it's too much for him, as well, but Mum only laughs and says he needs the exercise. I wish he'd leave it like it is, full of mossy stones and secret places.

C. V. Molesworth's house looks a lot like our place. Even the windows are like ours – which means that they're not exactly sparkling clean.

I still felt a bit guilty about the accident I *might* have caused, and looking at the next-door windows gave me a kind, neighbourly idea. I could wash them for C. V. Molesworth!

16 The Crescent
September 16

Dear P. S. McGinnity,

I can only assume that you find it amusing to hose a person through that person's bedroom window while the person is attempting to have a rest – on doctor's orders. I had not thought from the tone of your previous letter that you would be a spiteful person. I am shocked and saddened.

Apart from being soaked to the skin myself, there is also the matter of a wet quilt and mattress.

I wish Mr Thomas still lived next door. He would never, under any circumstances, have treated me in such a way. In fact, we never exchanged one single word on any subject whatsoever.

Yours faithfully,

C. V. Molesworth

C. V. Molesworth

"I thought that the window was closed," I said again. "I was only trying to be neighbourly and helpful."

Dad looked gloomy. "Now we'll be sued," he said.

"I could put the mattress outside to dry, hang out the quilt, and offer to do odd jobs," I suggested.

Mum nearly exploded. "We have enough odd jobs around *here* to take us into the next century!" (She'd just discovered that the whole house needed new wiring, and she was a bit tense.)

Dad thought for a moment. "P. S. can write an apology, and she can offer to pay the cleaning costs."

"I don't have enough money!" I yelled in alarm.

"Pen and paper, P. S.," Dad said sternly.

18 The Crescent
September 17

Dear C. V. Molesworth,

A misunderstanding on my part has occurred in the matter of your bedroom window. I thought it was shut. My intention was to clean it for you, not to soak you to the skin.

That's the truth. I am not spiteful, as you think. Mum and Dad will pay for any cleaning, but I hope it's not too much because they're worried about how much it's costing to fix up our place.

I don't want to move. I really love it here. I expect you did, too — before I moved in next door. I'm really sorry for my mistake.

Your unhappy neighbour,

P.S. McGinnity

P. S. McGinnity

"What have you been up to?" Mum asked. "You're a sight!"

I'd wriggled and pushed through a tangle of bushes growing along the fence, but it had been worth it. I'd found some lovely pink flowers.

"I think they're called dog-roses," Mum explained, which I thought was a strange name for them. "Let's find a vase."

"Half for you," I told her, "and half for C. V. Molesworth."

Mum looked uneasy. "I don't know, P. S. — maybe we should let sleeping dogs lie."

Dog roses? Sleeping dogs? With all this sudden talk about dogs, I actually forgot about C. V. Molesworth for a second and wondered if Mum was hinting at something. So far I'd never been allowed to have a dog, but maybe Mum had changed her mind, now that we had a big garden.

I looked hopeful, but she only said, "It's peaceful now. I'd like to keep it that way."

16 The Crescent
September 21

Dear P. S. McGinnity,

I was somewhat surprised to find that a
"gift" of my own roses had appeared on
my doorstep. I don't like people who
give with one hand and take with the
other. Stealing, I call it.

You are right. I did like it here
before you moved next door. Clearly,
things will never be the same again.
Now I wake up each morning wondering
what new disaster you are saving up for
me.

Your worried neighbour,

C. V. Molesworth

C. V. Molesworth

C. V. Molesworth's latest letter upset me a lot. She'd practically called me a thief! I went off and started to cry. I really hadn't known that those pink flowers had been growing through the fence from her place. As if I would have given them to her if I'd realised!

I decided to write one more letter and then follow Mr Thomas's example and never speak to C. V. Molesworth again. Who would want to?

18 The Crescent
September 22

Dear C. V. Molesworth,

I have made another mistake, just as I did with the windows. I thought those were our roses or I wouldn't have picked them. I wanted to make it up to you.

Mum was right. She said I should have "let sleeping dogs lie". I thought she might be changing her mind about getting a dog, but she meant that trying to be friends with you would only lead to more trouble.

It's probably best if we don't exchange another word, like you and Mr Thomas. That way nothing else can go wrong.

Your sad and silent neighbour,

P. S. McGinnity

P. S. McGinnity

Mum's magazine article was due. It had been difficult for her to find time to write while we were moving into our new house.

"Will you go to the post office for me, P. S.?" she asked. "You'll need to be quick. Oh, and here's some money. We need some milk as well."

I was on my way back when it happened. I had just passed Number 16 (somewhat cautiously), when a furry brown shape zoomed out the gate, closely followed by a woman waving a lead and shrieking, "Stop, Roly, stop!"

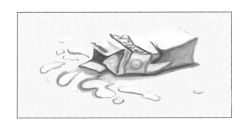

But the mysterious Roly was beyond stopping. He was on a collision course with my legs. Roly, the carton of milk and I all went down in a heap. Luckily for me it was a soft landing! Dad had spent all weekend digging the front garden before planting his new seedlings – which were now being watered by the garden sprinkler.

I looked up from my bed of squashed seedlings. Staring back down at me was the shocked, saddened and recently soaked resident from next door, C. V. Molesworth.

"P. S. McGinnity?" She rapped out my name suddenly.

"Y-y-yes," I stammered.

"What does the P. S. stand for?"

I felt myself blushing through the milk. "Petunia Sylvania," I muttered. "It's stupid. Just call me P. S."

"It's a perfectly good name," she retorted.

Then I remembered Dad telling me that attack is the best form of defence. "So, what does C. V. stand for?" I demanded, with as much dignity as I could muster, with milk dripping from the end of my nose.

Now *she* looked embarrassed. She didn't want to answer any more than I'd wanted to. There was a long pause. "Charity Victoria," she mumbled. "Fool of a name!"

"Charity is a perfectly good name, too," I said. I couldn't believe my eyes. C. V. Molesworth was actually blushing!

"Well, we'd better get you cleaned up, hadn't we," she said.

Much later, in dry clothes and after a long round of apologies from C. V. Molesworth, I found myself sitting on my neighbour's porch. By then she'd replaced Mum's carton of milk and even offered to help Dad replant the front garden. (He graciously declined.)

C. V. Molesworth's porch was beautiful. There were hanging baskets of leafy plants and pots of bright geraniums. We sat on old cane chairs with faded velvet cushions. Wind chimes tinkled softly in the breeze. And at my feet slept a worn-out brown puppy.

"I could guess from your letters that you wished you had a dog," C. V. Molesworth explained. "And that made me remember how much I used to enjoy having a dog around the place. I thought it would be good to have a watch-dog, too, now that I'm on my own. So I went to the pound and picked out Roly. I was just about to take him for a walk when he saw you go past and dashed away from me," she said. "I'm very sorry about all the trouble we caused."

I told her I was sorry about the trouble I'd caused her, too. "I rush into things without thinking. It's a bad habit."

"Well, I suppose we both know now how it feels to be knocked down, covered with milk, and soaked through to the skin," said C. V. Molesworth.

"With a vandalised garden to add to the matter," I said, trying not to laugh. But it was too late; a chuckle escaped from the corner of my mouth. To my surprise, C. V. Molesworth was trying not to laugh, too. So we both stopped trying and really roared!

"You do like dogs, P. S., don't you?" said C. V. Molesworth, when we had finally calmed down enough to speak.

"Yes, but Mum won't let me have one. She says she likes her home to be peaceful."

C. V. Molesworth's eyes twinkled. "With you around? She must be joking!"

I didn't mind her saying that now that we were friends.

C. V. Molesworth leaned slightly towards me. "I tell you what, P. S.; I'd love it if you'd come over sometimes and help me with Roly. He certainly needs some training, and he definitely likes you."

The only trouble is, Roly has become such a good watch-dog that he wants to scare *everyone* away from the place – even me!

"But where there's a will, there's a way," C. V. Molesworth says.

And I think she's right. We've worked out our "little" problems before – and I bet we can solve this one, too!

TITLES IN THE SERIES

SET 9A

Television Drama
Time for Sale
The Shady Deal
The Loch Ness Monster Mystery
Secrets of the Desert

SET 9B

To JJ From CC
Pandora's Box
The Birthday Disaster
The Song of the Mantis
Helping the Hoiho

SET 9C

Glumly
Rupert and the Griffin
The Tree, the Trunk, and the Tuba
Errol the Peril
Cassidy's Magic

SET 9D

Barney
Get a Grip, Pip!
Casey's Case
Dear Future
Strange Meetings

SET 10A

A Battle of Words
The Rainbow Solution
Fortune's Friend
Eureka
It's a Frog's Life

SET 10B

The Cat Burglar of Pethaven Drive
The Matchbox
In Search of the Great Bears
Many Happy Returns
Spider Relatives

SET 10C

Horrible Hank
Brian's Brilliant Career
Fernitickles
It's All in Your Mind,
    James Robert
Wing High, Gooftah

SET 10D

The Week of the Jellyhoppers
Timothy Whuffenpuffen-
    Whippersnapper
Timedetectors
Ryan's Dog Ringo
The Secret of Kiribu Tapu Lagoo